Angels are sent from heaven to remind us of the gifts we have in our family and friends and to keep us focused on the opportunity we are given to experience unconditional love through the connections we make. On the day when you most need it, and least expect it, you will be blessed by the guidance of an angel and touched by God's love.

Titles by Marci
Published by
Blue Mountain Arts®

Angels Are Everywhere!
Angels Bring a Message
of Hope Whenever It Is Needed

Friends Are Forever
A Gift of Inspirational Thoughts
to Thank You for Being
My Friend

10 Simple Things to Remember
An Inspiring Guide to
Understanding Life

To My Daughter
Love and Encouragement
to Carry with You on Your
Journey Through Life

To My Granddaughter
A Gift of Love and Wisdom
to Always Carry
in Your Heart

To My Mother
I Will Always Carry
Your Love in My Heart

To My Sister
A Gift of Love and Inspiration
to Thank You
for Being My Sister

To My Son
Love and Encouragement
to Carry with You on Your
Journey Through Life

You Are My "Once in a Lifetime"
I Will Always Love You

Angels Are Everywhere!

Angels Bring a Message
of Hope Whenever It Is Needed

Marci

Blue Mountain Press™
Boulder, Colorado

Dedicated to all those who have ever performed a random act of kindness. The love and caring you put into the world is surely the work of angels! God bless you!

Library of Congress Control Number: 2014939170
ISBN: 978-1-68088-220-9 (previously ISBN: 978-1-59842-827-8)

Children of the Inner Light is a registered trademark. Used under license.
Certain trademarks are used under license.

Printed in China.
First printing of this edition: 2018

♻ This book is printed on recycled paper.

This book is printed on paper that has been specially produced to be acid free (neutral pH) and contains no groundwood or unbleached pulp. It conforms with the requirements of the American National Standards Institute, Inc., so as to ensure that this book will last and be enjoyed by future generations.

Blue Mountain Arts, Inc.
P.O. Box 4549, Boulder, Colorado 80306

Contents

Introduction

Not too long ago I was reminded of why I do what I do. It was near Christmas. I was at the local mall to do a product signing. For the occasion, I had created a special Christmas ornament with my angel design and the words "Angels Are Everywhere!"

The signing was scheduled to last four hours, and I was a little tired. My life had been hectic over the last year with lots of stiff deadlines to meet. There was a short break in the flow of people, and my mind wandered to the projects waiting for me at home. I was working on a new line of journals, and I began to think about the "Friends" journal. In it, I had written, "If you have good friends, you have almost everything." How simple and how true, I thought. Then my mind turned to the next journal called "Faith." In that one, I had written, "Say two prayers: help and thank you." People would be reminded, I thought, of what it means to have faith... to pray for help, to let God decide what kind of help, and then to say "thank you" for His blessings every day.

Suddenly I was pulled away from my thoughts by a blond-haired woman with a sweet smile, who in a lovely voice asked, "Are you Marci?" When I answered "yes," she went on to say, "Oh, I am so happy to meet you. I love your work, especially your angel design." I told her it was my favorite too.

I became acutely aware of this woman's presence as she continued, "I know all about angels. I am a nurse." I immediately knew what she meant and nodded. We looked at each other knowingly as I thought of the miracles she had probably witnessed. Her blue eyes sparkled. We had made a wonderful connection with our conversation, and with the intense focus we shared, everything around me seemed to disappear. Then she spoke again: "On the day when you least expect it, and most need it, an angel will bring a message of hope." As she finished her words, my breath caught in my throat and tears welled up in my eyes. I stared at her for an uncomfortable moment, but her eyes never left mine. She was smiling. "How did you know what I wrote in my new angel journal?" I asked. "I am working on it now, and no one has ever seen it." She didn't answer. At that moment, I felt a tap on my shoulder, and I turned to respond. When I turned back, the woman was gone.

This is only one of my "angel stories," as these events have become routine for me. What is not "routine," though, is my reaction to each occurrence, which is to stop in my tracks and say a prayer of gratitude for another "message of hope." My wish for you is that you will begin to record your own angel stories and delight in sharing them with others.

Enjoy,

Marci

Angels

Are Everywhere!

Sometimes we feel that we are all alone, as life brings us challenges to overcome and hardships to bear. But when we least expect it, help can appear. It may be a kind word from a stranger or a phone call at just the right time, and we are suddenly surrounded with the loving grace of God. Miracles happen every day because angels are everywhere.

Hope Is a Gift...

Hope

Hope is believing that miracles are possible!

That We Give to Ourselves

Oftentimes our path seems to be filled with roadblocks, and we wonder why life is so difficult. Things happen that leave us feeling as though we have little control over our circumstances. This is a time to remember that hope is a gift we can give to ourselves... When we choose this attitude and tap into our inner reserves, we are rewarded with the knowledge of what we have learned in life. The decision to look forward, stay positive, and remain hopeful is a key that unlocks the door to possibilities and, when shared, returns to renew the spirit.

Everything Happens

This Way Home

for a Reason

So often we wonder about the "whys" in life... "Why did this happen?" "Why me?" "Why now?" But there is a secret that wise men know... Bumps in the road are an inevitable part of life that soften us, make us grow, and bestow upon us the virtue of compassion. Often it is only with the passing of time that it becomes clear that the cloud really did have a silver lining, and now we have wisdom, strength, and hope to share. And at last, we understand the true meaning of the phrase "Everything happens for a reason."

The Miracle

In childhood, we do not understand the gifts wrapped up in a greater plan... but time and the living of life carve into our souls an attitude of acceptance and understanding. Adulthood brings an appreciation of all the gifts we've been given and a realization that some of the most valuable gifts are the ones we had labeled as losses. The universe has chosen for us — or perhaps we have selected for ourselves — the path we need to become whole.

Sometimes we follow... sometimes we resist, only to circle back around to the lessons left unlearned. One day... after a big storm... a rainbow will appear. We will find the sky is bright with a beautiful realization that everything "is as it should be."

Simple miracles are all around us and confirm that there is so much more to life than we can see. Be open to the guidance of an angel.

FAITH

HOPE

LOVE

May you be blessed with all the good things in life... faith, hope, love, and the blessing of family and friends. If you have these things, whatever challenges life brings, you will get through. Your faith will light your path... hope will keep you strong... the love you give to others will bring you joy... and your family and friends will remind you of what is important.

Our Friends Are a Blessing...

Time Spent
With Friends
Creates Lifelong
Sweet Memories

Friendship is one of life's greatest treasures, and it is a gift that lasts a lifetime. We create bonds during times in our lives when our beliefs and our experiences are shaping who we are. Those bonds cannot be broken by the passing of time, even when life gets so busy that we lose touch. Let friends know that you think of them often... and they will always have a special place in your heart.

Friendship Means...

Friendship means never having to face the challenges of life alone.

Friendship means sharing a closeness of spirit that gives life meaning.

Friendship means having a witness to life's tiny, special moments that are so much better when shared.

Friendship means always having someone there to hold your hand, to share your triumphs, and to shine a light of hope when the road gets dark.

Friendship means that there is someone who understands where you've been, Knows where you want to go, and accepts you for who you are.

A Good Friendship
Brightens Every Day

Our Families
Are a Blessing...

Time Spent With
Loved Ones Creates an
Everlasting Bond

Families are special creations made up of people who love each other and are tied together with threads of common experience, memories, and values. Some families we are born into... some families we choose... all families are a blessing every day.

Family Means...

Family means having someone to give you a hug when you need one.

Family means having someone to love you through good times and bad.

Family means having someone to share life's joys and dry the tears through life's sorrows.

Family means that someone is there to shine a light on the path ahead... and shed some light on the path behind.

Family means that there are people who will always love you no matter what.

The background consists of the word "love" written repeatedly in various styles around the border of a heart shape.

Love Is a Blessing...

Love

Love Is the Greatest Gift of All

Love answers the question "Why are we here?" Love is a gift that we can choose every day. We can remember to tell those most important to us how we feel... we can show kindness to others, knowing that we have made a difference. We can remember to receive love as it is offered. We can pray, making that connection with God who is all love.

Love Means...

Love means accepting the love of others as they give it. This is the way to experience unconditional love.

Love means giving all you have and asking for little in return. It is sharing the joys but also supporting another through sorrow and spiritual growth.

Love means acknowledging that we always have a choice. Love is not a feeling... love is an action... love is a choice.

Love means remembering that when you're tempted to say one more thing... let it be "I love you."

Love means living in a way that demonstrates a belief in another's goodness... always positive, always encouraging, and always full of faith.

Faith Will Light Your Path...

We Walk by Faith

Faith is the assurance of things not seen. It is knowing that God is always by your side through all of life's journey and guiding your steps every day. It is believing that a power greater than ourselves knows what is best for us and those around us. It is the foundation that we come to rely on as we take our journey through life.

When you Question God's Plan, Remember These Things

Life is a path filled with many experiences. If they were all painless, we would not have a way to measure our joy.

Our losses lead to an understanding of what it means to feel grateful in a way that reaches deep into our hearts.

Our mistakes show us that only God is perfect... that we are human and need each other... and that through that need comes the connection that allows us to experience selfless love.

Often it is through our struggles that we gain the most understanding. We learn about who we are, what we believe, and what is really important through everyday living. When we meet the challenge to change and grow spiritually, accepting our joys and our sorrows with gratitude, we become wise.

Wisdom for
Your Journey

FAITH ♥
HOPE ♥
LOVE ♥

As You Follow
Life's Path,
Remember...

No matter where life takes you or what path you choose, you will always meet challenges. That is the way life is. There are no guarantees, and no matter how many things you do right or how many rules you follow, there will always be that fork in the road that makes you choose between this way or that. Whenever you meet this place, remember these things: You are loved... love will sustain you. You are strong... prayer will get you through anything.

God Holds Your Heart in His Hands

The world today gives us many challenges. We try to juggle so many different things, wanting to give pieces of ourselves to our jobs, our friends, and our families, and through it all, we find that our days are filled with worry. We must remember to live each day "one at a time"... to let go of things we cannot change... and to keep in mind that God is always with us as He holds our hearts in His hands.

Some things just take time to work out, some things take prayer and a change in attitude, and some things require an action on our part. You will take the right path and once again know serenity.

God loves you♥ God loves you ♥ God loves you ♥ ♥ God loves you ♥

Remember the
Power of Prayer...

There Is Always
Hope Because
There Is Prayer

Just when we think all hope is lost, grace comes in like a breeze with a gentle reminder of the power of prayer. When we pray, we open our hearts to the many blessings available to us. When we remember that our needs are always taken care of, we will experience the power of prayer.

Prayer is a gift. It is a choice we make to open ourselves to God's love that is always there for us. When we make this decision, we demonstrate our faith in a greater plan. May faith show you the way... may hope shine a light on your path... and may prayer be the gift that always starts your day.

Guardian angel, light my way.
Please be with me through the day.
Remind me I am in your care,
and should help be needed,
you will be there.

Think of
Each Day as...

a New Start

Sometimes we make mistakes... that is a part of our nature. We fall down because we are human and imperfect. Fortunately, each day is a chance to begin again, to wipe the slate clean, and to remember that today is the only day that exists. The past is gone... tomorrow is in the future... but today is a chance for a new start!

There are times in our lives when happiness seems to elude us. We want more... We wish we were further along in our lives... We desire better relationships... We try to push ourselves beyond where we are at the moment. Sometimes, all that is needed is a change of mind... a change called "acceptance." With this change there comes a sense of peace and a sudden realization that a "shift in thinking" has brought us the very things we were looking for all along!

Acceptance
Is the Key

Life is a process, not an event. All that you experience is necessary for your understanding.

If you have learned something from every experience, there should be no regrets. If you understand that learning is a process, there are no wrong decisions.

Fighting against the way things are causes most personal suffering — acceptance is the path to serenity. One of life's paradoxes: acceptance creates the fertile soil for change.

Life is a journey home. As we grow and mature and travel the unknown forests, we search, like Dorothy, for Oz — looking for wisdom, courage, and love. We meet demons and dragons and somehow overcome them all. What ordinary people call coincidence has been our guide. Finally, after great struggle, we realize we are already and always home. We snap our ruby slippers and revel in the acknowledgment that all we have needed in our lives has always been there.

Happiness Is a Choice... Pass It On!

You can make the decision to "be happy" each day.

Remember that happiness is contagious. Make someone smile, and the good feelings come right back to you.

Realize that true happiness and purpose will be found in relationships with each other and with God. It is often through sharing your gifts and talents that your path in life will become clear.

We each have a chance every day to brighten the life of another. It can be a kind smile... a simple hello... shared inspiration... or an unexpected gesture to let someone know that their being in the world makes a difference. When good things come into your life, be inspired to brighten the day of another.

Give away some courage every day! When you encourage another to "keep going," "hang in there," or "believe in your dreams," you will find an unending source of happiness.

Hope is a gift from God. It is a state of mind in which we remember that our needs are always taken care of and miracles are before us every day. Hope is a gift that we can give to others as we encourage their dreams and comfort their sorrows.

Angels are at work in our lives
every day... watching over us,
prompting us to be compassionate,
reminding us to pray, and sometimes
working through others to bring an
unexpected kindness that makes us
stop and realize just how wonderful
and giving the human spirit is!

Listen for that voice inside guiding you toward the right thing to do, the right path to travel, and the knowledge of what will bring you happiness and fulfillment. That voice is very quiet, like a whisper. Over time, and mostly through the challenges in life, you will learn to hear it more clearly. Whenever you feel that tug to do something new, help someone in need, or share what you have learned, listen carefully.

Live your beliefs... and be a powerful example of love in the world.

Be compassionate... Life is difficult, and people are often working through private battles.

Demonstrate acts of kindness... "Little ones" are watching you and learning about compassion.

Encourage someone today... The words "everything will be okay" can lighten the heart of another. Share love... there is an endless supply.

Be hopeful... your attitude will uplift the spirit of another.

God's Plan Will Unfold With Perfect Timing

If only we could see the big picture, we would know that in the grand scheme of things "It's all good!" But we can't see the future... so we must rely on faith and the assurance that comes with it that life is unfolding according to a divine plan.

Remember that timing is important. There is a right time for everything, and the universe will unfold its magnificent plan in a time that is not ours to decide. We must have faith that a power greater than ourselves knows what is best for us... and when. It is often only when we look back at the path behind us that we realize the perfect timing of our journey... and we begin to understand the meaning of gratitude.

Gratitude Is a
Gift You Can
Choose Each Day...

Give Thanks
for Each Day
in Advance

One of life's greatest gifts is gratitude, and it is free for the choosing. As we practice seeing life in a positive light, we become able to experience all the good things that are present in our lives and let go of the past. With daily thanksgiving, we realize that we're on the path to serenity.

Letting go of the past is one of the most difficult things we have to do. When you find yourself holding on to a situation you cannot change, remember these things...

There are many things in life we have no control of, but we do have a choice about how we see them.

Roadblocks are obstacles that push us back on track.

Focusing inward on our choices instead of trying to move mountains frees up energy that turns roadblocks into steppingstones.

Do the best you can for today, letting faith be the candle that guides your way.

Hold positive thoughts in your heart and be at peace...

Peace in Knowing who you are.

Peace in Knowing what you believe.

Peace as you begin each day, always looking forward with hope and optimism.

Peace as you look back at your life, accepting that every step was for the greater good.

Peace as you sleep, Knowing that your soul is in the care of the angels.

Angels Have So Many...

Angels Are Everywhere

Important Lessons to Share

Don't worry... big problems can be solved in small steps.

When you are still, the gentle voice from within will guide you... listen carefully.

Remember to pray, and let God take the burden of worry from your heart.

Accept that we each learn life's lessons in our own way.

Find Your Inner Strength...

an Angel Will Show You the Way

It is often through our deepest pain that we experience the greatest times of spiritual growth. We are called to be more than we ever imagined, and as a result, we discover an inner strength that we may not have known existed. When we get through difficult times, we come through as a stronger person. We now have important experiences to share with others, as real wisdom is always gained the hard way.

There are times in our lives when we face a hardship that we do not think we can bear. We wonder "Why?" and we look for a reason to help make sense of it all. Sometimes all we can do is try to come to a place of acceptance and reach out to others who understand what we've been through. Often it is then — as we share our wisdom, strength, and hope — that we get a small glimpse of a larger plan... one that enables us to feel connected... one that shows us that love blesses the giver and the receiver... and one that allows us to see how really strong we are.

Get Through
Hard Times
with

GOD

Give to others the very things you most need... support, encouragement, and hope. Giving always goes in a circle and returns to renew the spirit.

Open your heart to the grace of God through prayer. When you ask for help, you create within yourself the conditions to receive God's love.

Do the best you can for today. Do not ask more of yourself than you can handle today. You are a child of God, and you will be cared for in a way you may only understand tomorrow.

Believe in Miracles...

Miracles Happen
Every Day
When We Believe

We may not always know the right thing to do or the right path to take, but faith will show us the way. Remember that we are never alone, as God is always there to answer prayers and send us the help that we need. Have faith, knowing that things generally work out as they should.

Celebrate
Life...

Hope Is a Gift
to Share

Every day is a gift and a reason to celebrate when we remember to be grateful for the things that are really important. Life brings us joys and sorrows, struggles and triumphs, but it is our simple blessings that will get us through. Faith will light your path, hope will keep you strong, love will bring you your greatest joys, and your friendships will remind you that every day is a reason to celebrate.

You Deserve the Best!

May all the good things you have brought to others be returned to you.

May your steps be guided through all of life's challenges and your heart remember its true calling.

May your future be filled with love and acceptance.

May God's grace find its way to you every day... protect you from worry... and fill your heart with unshakable faith in difficult times.

May hope be a constant in your life... a gift to yourself and others.

May love warm your heart every day.

God Bless
You and
Keep You...

Angels Bring
a Message of Hope
Whenever It
Is Needed

On the days when you need inspiration, I pray you are blessed with these understandings and that you always keep them in your heart.

You are one of God's perfect creations, and you have everything you need to fulfill your life's purpose.

You are never alone... on the day when you need it most, an angel will send a message of hope. Angels are everywhere.

You are goodness and light, and when you share that part of yourself, you will discover pure joy.

The Road
of Life

If All Else Fails
Pet the Dog

All Paths Lead
to Home

Has Many Turns

Sometimes the road of life takes us to a place we had planned... Sometimes it shows us a surprise around the bend we could never have anticipated. We make decisions based on the information we have... We accept the ups and downs as they come... We live "one day at a time." But often we find it is only when we look back that we can see that what we had thought was a "wrong turn" has brought us to exactly the right place and every step was a right one after all!

As You Follow
Your Path,
Remember...

This Is the
Way Home

Live your faith... your example will light a path for others to follow.

Be kind... Kindness is a beautiful gift. The love and caring you give to others will be a confirmation that angels are everywhere.

Always choose love... Understand that love and fear are contradictions.

Recognize love by the paradox that it is both powerful and gentle at the same time...

When things go wrong, always come back to knowing that a greater plan than you ever dreamed for yourself has been laid out for you.

Remember that by your actions you can uplift the spirit of another, and when you are both having a rough day, this is the fastest route to happiness!

Be grateful for the little things in life that are free. Make a list, and add to it each morning.

Accept that your family, your
friendships, and the love you find
are the things you will look back
on one day and realize that
all of your dreams have come true!

A Blessing
for Your
Journey...

This
♥ Way ♥
♥ Home ♥

God Bless You

May the hand of God bless you... guide you... provide for you... give you hope when days are long... give you patience when things go wrong... fill you with joy for the little things... and be with you throughout your journey, wherever it may take you.

Your
Guardian
Angel...

Is Always
by Your Side
to Bless You

May your guardian angel stay by your side... to bring you inspiration when life gets you down... to fill your heart with determination when life puts obstacles in your path... and to shower you with grace to nurture your spiritual growth as you travel your path through life. May your angel wrap you in God's love every day!

About Marci

Marci began her career by hand painting floral designs on clothing. No one was more surprised than she was when one day, in a single burst of inspiration and a completely new and different art style, her delightful characters sprang from her pen! "Their wild and crazy hair is a sign of strength," she thought, "and their crooked little smiles are endearing." She quickly identified the charming characters as Mother, Daughter, Sister, Father, Son, Friend, and so on until all the people and places in life were filled. Then, with her own loved ones in mind, she wrote a true and special sentiment to each one. This would be the beginning of a wonderful success story, which today still finds Marci writing each and every one of her verses in this same personal way.

Marci is a self-taught artist who has always enjoyed writing and art. She is thrilled to see how her delightful characters and universal messages of love have touched the hearts and lives of people everywhere. Her distinctive designs can also be found on Blue Mountain Arts greeting cards, calendars, bookmarks, and other gift items.

To learn more about Marci, look for Children of the Inner Light on Facebook or visit her website: WWW.MARCIonline.com.